We hope this book has been informative and helpful on your journey to understanding and celebrating older adults. Thank you for your interest and support!

Title: The Role of Mining Pools in 51% Attack Prevention
Subtitle: Strategies and Best Practices

Series: Defending Bitcoin: A Comprehensive Guide to 51% Attack Prevention
By S. J. Matthews

"Bitcoin is a remarkable cryptographic achievement and the ability to create something that is not duplicable in the digital world has enormous value."
Eric Schmidt, Former CEO of Google

"Bitcoin is a technological tour de force."
Bill Gates, Co-Founder of Microsoft

"Bitcoin is the beginning of something great: a currency without a government, something necessary and imperative."
Nassim Taleb, Author of "The Black Swan"

"Bitcoin is a remarkable cryptographic achievement... The ability to create something which is not duplicable in the digital world has enormous value."
Roger Ver, Bitcoin Investor and Entrepreneur

"Bitcoin is a remarkable cryptographic achievement and the ability to create something that is not duplicable in the digital world has enormous value."
Peter Thiel, Co-Founder of PayPal

"Bitcoin is a very exciting development, it might lead to a world currency. I think over the next decade it will grow to become one of the most important ways to pay for things and transfer assets."
Kim Dotcom, Founder of Megaupload

"Bitcoin is a protocol that could change the world, like the web did. Don't miss out."
Andreas Antonopoulos, Bitcoin Educator and Author

"Bitcoin is better than currency in that you don't have to be physically in the same place and, of course, for large transactions, currency can get pretty inconvenient."
Bill Gates, Co-Founder of Microsoft

Table of Contents

Introduction 7

Understanding the importance of securing your Bitcoin wallet 7

Common types of wallet vulnerabilities 10

Overview of the book's contents 13

Chapter 1: Types of Bitcoin Wallets 16

Overview of Bitcoin wallets 16

Hot wallets vs. cold wallets 18

Software wallets vs. hardware wallets 23

Choosing the right wallet for your needs 26

Chapter 2: Securing Your Bitcoin Wallet 28

Creating a strong password 28

Two-factor authentication 30

Multisignature wallets 32

Seed phrases and recovery phrases 35

Chapter 3: Best Practices for Bitcoin Storage 37

Avoiding online wallets and exchanges 37

Keeping your wallet software and hardware up-to-date 40

Backing up your wallet 43

Keeping your private keys secure 45

Chapter 4: Protecting Against Common Scams and Attacks 48

Phishing attacks and how to avoid them *48*

Malware and other types of attacks *51*

Avoiding public Wi-Fi networks *54*

Recognizing and avoiding Ponzi schemes and other scams

.... *57*

Chapter 5: Recovering from Wallet Theft or Loss.. 60

Steps to take if your wallet is hacked or stolen *60*

Recovering from a lost or damaged hardware wallet ... *63*

Preparing for the worst-case scenario *67*

Dealing with insurance and law enforcement *70*

Conclusion **74**

Review of the book's key takeaways *74*

Final thoughts on Bitcoin wallet security *78*

Encouragement to take action and protect your Bitcoin

holdings *82*

Key Terms and Definitions **85**

Supporting Materials **87**

Introduction

Understanding the importance of securing your Bitcoin wallet

Bitcoin is a decentralized digital currency that operates on a peer-to-peer network. It has grown in popularity and adoption over the past decade, with its value soaring to new heights. However, with the rise of Bitcoin and other cryptocurrencies comes the increased risk of cyber attacks and theft. Bitcoin wallets, like traditional bank accounts, hold your digital assets and are the target of many hacking attempts. In this chapter, we'll explore the importance of securing your Bitcoin wallet, the risks involved, and the best practices to keep your assets safe.

The Importance of Bitcoin Wallet Security:

Bitcoin is stored in wallets, which can be digital or physical. Wallets are essentially software programs that store private keys that enable the owner to access and spend their Bitcoins. Wallets are the gatekeepers to your funds, and securing them is critical. A compromised wallet could mean the loss of your assets and sensitive information.

The risks involved in storing Bitcoin are unique compared to traditional currencies. Since Bitcoin is decentralized, there is no central authority responsible for its security. As a result, it's essential to take extra precautions to protect your assets.

One of the most significant risks to Bitcoin wallets is hacking. Cybercriminals have developed sophisticated methods to steal private keys, including phishing scams, malware, and social engineering tactics. Additionally, lost or stolen wallets are a common occurrence, which can be catastrophic if the owner doesn't have backups.

Another risk is human error. Forgetting passwords, misplacing private keys, and other errors can lead to the loss of your Bitcoins. And since transactions on the Bitcoin network are irreversible, there is no way to recover lost funds.

Best Practices for Securing Your Bitcoin Wallet:

To mitigate these risks, there are several best practices you can follow to secure your Bitcoin wallet. One of the most important is to use a hardware wallet. Hardware wallets are physical devices that store your private keys offline, making them less vulnerable to hacking attempts. You can also use a multisignature wallet that requires multiple private keys to access the wallet, adding an extra layer of security.

Creating a strong password is another critical step. Avoid using easy-to-guess passwords, and don't use the same password for multiple accounts. Two-factor authentication is also a must, requiring a second authentication factor, such as a text message or biometric verification, to log in.

Backing up your wallet is also essential. Ensure that you have a backup of your private keys in a secure location, preferably in multiple locations. Consider using a passphrase, which is a series of words used to encrypt your private keys.

Conclusion:

In conclusion, securing your Bitcoin wallet is essential to protect your assets and personal information. Understanding the risks involved and implementing best practices can go a long way in preventing theft and loss. In the next chapters, we'll explore different types of wallets and the best practices for securing them.

Common types of wallet vulnerabilities

Bitcoin wallets are software programs that store private keys, enabling users to access and spend their Bitcoins. While Bitcoin wallets are designed to be secure, they are not invulnerable to attacks. Cybercriminals are continually looking for vulnerabilities in wallets to steal private keys and access funds. In this chapter, we'll explore the common types of wallet vulnerabilities and how to protect against them.

1. Online Wallets:

Online wallets, also known as web wallets, are wallets that store private keys on a remote server that is managed by a third-party provider. While they offer convenience and accessibility, online wallets are susceptible to hacking attacks. Cybercriminals can exploit vulnerabilities in the provider's system, such as weak passwords or security flaws, to gain unauthorized access to the wallet.

To protect against this vulnerability, it's essential to choose a reputable and secure provider for your online wallet. Research the provider's security measures and read reviews from other users. Additionally, avoid using public Wi-Fi networks when accessing your online wallet, as these networks are often unsecured and easy to hack.

2. Mobile Wallets:

Mobile wallets are applications that run on mobile devices, such as smartphones or tablets. They offer convenience and ease of use, but they are also vulnerable to attacks. Cybercriminals can exploit vulnerabilities in the mobile operating system or the wallet application itself to access private keys.

To protect against this vulnerability, it's important to keep your mobile device and wallet application up-to-date with the latest security patches and updates. Additionally, avoid downloading wallet applications from third-party app stores or untrusted sources, as these can be infected with malware or other types of malicious software.

3. Hardware Wallets:

Hardware wallets are physical devices that store private keys offline, making them less vulnerable to hacking attacks. However, they are not invulnerable. Cybercriminals can exploit vulnerabilities in the hardware wallet's firmware or other components to access private keys.

To protect against this vulnerability, it's important to choose a reputable and secure hardware wallet provider. Research the provider's security measures and read reviews from other users. Additionally, keep your hardware wallet up-to-date with the latest firmware and security updates.

4. Social Engineering:

Social engineering is a tactic used by cybercriminals to manipulate individuals into revealing sensitive information, such as private keys. They may use techniques such as phishing scams, where they impersonate a trusted entity, or pretexting, where they create a false sense of trust to trick individuals into revealing private keys.

To protect against this vulnerability, it's important to be aware of social engineering tactics and avoid disclosing sensitive information to untrusted sources. Additionally, use two-factor authentication and other security measures to prevent unauthorized access to your wallet.

Conclusion:

In conclusion, Bitcoin wallets are vulnerable to a range of attacks and vulnerabilities. Understanding these vulnerabilities and taking steps to protect against them is critical to ensure the security of your Bitcoins. In the next chapters, we'll explore the best practices for securing different types of Bitcoin wallets.

Overview of the book's contents

In this book, we explore the legal and regulatory implications of 51% attacks on the Bitcoin network, including how different jurisdictions have responded to such attacks and how they may be prevented in the future. We also delve into the best practices for securing Bitcoin wallets, as well as strategies for preventing common types of scams and attacks.

Overview of the Book's Contents:

Chapter 1: Types of Bitcoin Wallets

In Chapter 1, we provide an overview of Bitcoin wallets and explore the different types of wallets available, including hot wallets, cold wallets, software wallets, and hardware wallets. We discuss the advantages and disadvantages of each type of wallet and provide guidance on choosing the right wallet for your needs.

Chapter 2: Securing Your Bitcoin Wallet

In Chapter 2, we delve into the best practices for securing your Bitcoin wallet. We cover topics such as creating a strong password, using two-factor authentication, and setting up a multisignature wallet. We also explore the importance of seed phrases and recovery phrases and provide guidance on how to use them effectively.

Chapter 3: Best Practices for Bitcoin Storage

In Chapter 3, we discuss the best practices for storing your Bitcoins, including avoiding online wallets and exchanges, keeping your wallet software and hardware up-to-date, and backing up your wallet. We also explore the importance of keeping your private keys secure and provide guidance on how to do so effectively.

Chapter 4: Protecting Against Common Scams and Attacks

In Chapter 4, we provide strategies for protecting against common types of scams and attacks, including phishing attacks, malware, public Wi-Fi networks, and Ponzi schemes. We also discuss the importance of recognizing and avoiding scams and provide guidance on how to do so effectively.

Chapter 5: Recovering from Wallet Theft or Loss

In Chapter 5, we explore the steps to take if your wallet is hacked or stolen, including recovering from a lost or damaged hardware wallet, preparing for the worst-case scenario, and dealing with insurance and law enforcement. We also provide guidance on how to minimize the risk of theft or loss in the first place.

Conclusion:

In conclusion, this book provides a comprehensive guide to securing your Bitcoin wallet and preventing common types of scams and attacks. It also explores the legal and regulatory implications of 51% attacks on the Bitcoin network and how to prevent them in the future. We hope that the information and guidance provided in this book will help you protect your Bitcoin holdings and enjoy the benefits of this exciting and innovative technology.

Chapter 1: Types of Bitcoin Wallets
Overview of Bitcoin wallets

A Bitcoin wallet is a digital wallet that allows you to store, send, and receive Bitcoins. It is similar to a physical wallet in that it allows you to store currency, but instead of holding paper bills, it stores digital coins. There are several types of Bitcoin wallets, each with its own advantages and disadvantages.

Hot Wallets vs. Cold Wallets:

One way to categorize Bitcoin wallets is by their connection to the internet. Hot wallets are connected to the internet, while cold wallets are not. Hot wallets are generally more convenient to use, as they allow you to access your Bitcoins from anywhere with an internet connection. However, they are also more vulnerable to hacking and other security risks, as they are constantly connected to the internet. Cold wallets, on the other hand, are more secure, as they are not connected to the internet. However, they are less convenient to use, as you need to physically connect them to a device with internet access to send or receive Bitcoins.

Software Wallets vs. Hardware Wallets:

Another way to categorize Bitcoin wallets is by the type of device they are stored on. Software wallets are digital wallets that are stored on a device such as a smartphone, tablet, or computer. They are generally free to use and easy to set up, but they are also more vulnerable to hacking and other security risks, as they are stored on devices that are connected to the internet. Hardware wallets, on the other hand, are physical devices that are specifically designed to store Bitcoins. They are generally more expensive than software wallets, but they are also more secure, as they are not connected to the internet and are designed to protect your private keys from hacking and other security risks.

Choosing the Right Wallet for Your Needs:

Choosing the right Bitcoin wallet for your needs depends on several factors, including your level of technical expertise, your budget, and your security needs. If you are new to Bitcoin and just getting started, a software wallet may be a good choice, as it is free and easy to set up. However, if you have a large amount of Bitcoins or are concerned about security, a hardware wallet may be a better choice, as it offers greater protection against hacking and other security risks.

In the next section, we will explore the different types of Bitcoin wallets in more detail, including their features, advantages, and disadvantages. We will also provide guidance on how to choose the right Bitcoin wallet for your needs.

Hot wallets vs. cold wallets

When it comes to Bitcoin wallets, one of the most important decisions you will make is whether to use a hot wallet or a cold wallet. Hot wallets and cold wallets have different advantages and disadvantages, and choosing the right type of wallet for your needs is essential to ensuring the security of your Bitcoin holdings.

Hot Wallets:

A hot wallet is a Bitcoin wallet that is connected to the internet. This type of wallet is generally more convenient to use than a cold wallet, as it allows you to access your Bitcoins from anywhere with an internet connection. There are several types of hot wallets, including desktop wallets, mobile wallets, and web wallets.

Desktop wallets are software wallets that are downloaded and installed on your computer. They offer a higher level of security than web wallets, as your private keys are stored on your own device rather than on a third-party server. However, they are still vulnerable to hacking and other security risks, as they are connected to the internet.

Mobile wallets are similar to desktop wallets, but are designed for use on mobile devices such as smartphones and tablets. They offer a high level of convenience, as you can access your Bitcoins on the go, but they are also vulnerable to hacking and other security risks, as they are connected to the internet.

Web wallets are Bitcoin wallets that are hosted by third-party service providers. They are generally the easiest type of wallet to use, as they require no software installation and can be accessed from any device with an internet connection. However, they are also the least secure type of wallet, as your private keys are stored on a third-party server that is vulnerable to hacking and other security risks.

Cold Wallets:

A cold wallet is a Bitcoin wallet that is not connected to the internet. This type of wallet is generally considered to be the most secure type of Bitcoin wallet, as it offers a high level of protection against hacking and other security risks. There are several types of cold wallets, including paper wallets, hardware wallets, and offline wallets.

Paper wallets are Bitcoin wallets that are printed on paper. They are generally the cheapest type of wallet to use, as they require no special software or hardware. However, they are also the least convenient type of wallet to use, as you need to manually enter your private keys every time you want to send or receive Bitcoins.

Hardware wallets are physical devices that are specifically designed to store Bitcoins. They offer a high level of security, as they are not connected to the internet and are designed to protect your private keys from hacking and other security risks. However, they are also the most expensive type of wallet to use, as they require the purchase of a physical device.

Offline wallets are Bitcoin wallets that are stored on a device that is not connected to the internet. They offer a high level of security, as they are not vulnerable to hacking and other security risks. However, they are also less convenient to use than other types of wallets, as you need to physically connect them to a device with internet access to send or receive Bitcoins.

Choosing the Right Wallet for Your Needs:

When choosing a Bitcoin wallet, it is important to consider your own security needs and level of technical expertise. If you are new to Bitcoin and just getting started, a hot wallet such as a web wallet or mobile wallet may be a good choice, as it is easy to use and requires no special software or hardware. However, if you have a large amount of Bitcoins or are concerned about security, a cold wallet such as a hardware wallet or paper wallet may be a better choice, as it offers greater protection against hacking and theft. Cold wallets are also referred to as offline wallets since they are not connected to the internet, which reduces the risk of unauthorized access. In contrast, hot wallets are always connected to the internet, making them more susceptible to hacking and malware attacks. It is important to note that both hot and cold wallets have their own advantages and disadvantages, and the choice ultimately depends on your specific needs and preferences. Let's explore the differences between hot and cold wallets in more detail.

Hot wallets, as mentioned earlier, are connected to the internet and are therefore more vulnerable to security breaches. There are various types of hot wallets, including web wallets, mobile wallets, and desktop wallets. Web wallets are online platforms that allow users to store and manage their Bitcoins through a web browser. Mobile wallets are applications that can be installed on a smartphone, providing easy access to Bitcoin funds on-the-go. Desktop wallets, on the other hand, are software applications that can be downloaded and installed on a computer. While hot wallets are convenient to use and offer quick access to your funds, they may not provide the same level of security as cold wallets.

In contrast, cold wallets are offline storage devices that are not connected to the internet. There are different types of cold wallets, including hardware wallets and paper wallets. Hardware wallets are small, portable devices that can be connected to a computer or smartphone to manage Bitcoin funds securely. These wallets generate private keys offline and store them in a secure environment, making it difficult for hackers to access them. Paper wallets, on the other hand, involve printing out a physical copy of your private key and keeping it in a safe place. While cold wallets offer greater security than hot wallets, they may not be as convenient to use and may require more technical knowledge to set up and manage.

Software wallets vs. hardware wallets

When it comes to Bitcoin wallets, there are two main categories: software wallets and hardware wallets. In this section, we will explore the differences between the two and the advantages and disadvantages of each.

Software wallets, also known as digital wallets or online wallets, are software programs that store your private keys on your computer or mobile device. These wallets can be further categorized into two subcategories: desktop wallets and mobile wallets.

Desktop wallets are software programs that you can download and install on your computer. They provide you with complete control over your private keys and allow you to store multiple cryptocurrencies in a single wallet. Some examples of desktop wallets include Electrum, Exodus, and Bitcoin Core.

Mobile wallets, as the name suggests, are wallets that you can install on your smartphone. They offer the convenience of accessing your Bitcoins on-the-go, making them a popular choice for users who frequently use their mobile devices. Some examples of mobile wallets include Mycelium, Bread, and Edge.

Software wallets offer several advantages over hardware wallets. Firstly, they are typically free to download and use, which makes them a cost-effective option for users. Secondly, they are easy to use and require minimal technical knowledge. Thirdly, they offer flexibility and convenience, as you can access your Bitcoins from anywhere with an internet connection.

However, software wallets also have some disadvantages. Firstly, they are vulnerable to hacking and malware attacks, especially if you store your private keys on a device that is connected to the internet. Secondly, if your device is lost or stolen, you may lose access to your Bitcoins if you do not have a backup of your private keys. Thirdly, if you download a wallet from an untrusted source, you risk downloading malware that could steal your private keys and access your Bitcoins.

Hardware wallets, on the other hand, are physical devices that are designed to store your private keys offline. These devices are typically USB drives that you can connect to your computer or smartphone. Examples of hardware wallets include Trezor, Ledger Nano S, and KeepKey.

Hardware wallets offer several advantages over software wallets. Firstly, they provide the highest level of security for your Bitcoins since your private keys are stored offline. This makes them virtually immune to hacking and malware attacks. Secondly, they offer better protection against physical theft since the device must be physically accessed to access the private keys. Thirdly, they are user-friendly and easy to use, even for users with limited technical knowledge.

However, hardware wallets also have some disadvantages. Firstly, they are not free and can be relatively expensive compared to software wallets. Secondly, they are less convenient than software wallets, as you must physically connect the device to your computer or smartphone to access your Bitcoins. Thirdly, if you lose or damage the device, you may lose access to your Bitcoins if you do not have a backup of your private keys.

In summary, both software and hardware wallets have their own advantages and disadvantages. Software wallets offer flexibility and convenience, while hardware wallets offer the highest level of security. The choice between the two ultimately depends on your security needs and preferences. If you are concerned about security and have a significant amount of Bitcoins, a hardware wallet may be a better option. If you are a casual user and value convenience, a software wallet may be a better option.

Choosing the right wallet for your needs

Choosing the right Bitcoin wallet can be a daunting task, especially for those new to the cryptocurrency space. With so many options available, it is important to carefully consider your needs and preferences to select the wallet that best fits your requirements.

First, you should consider your security needs. If you hold a large amount of Bitcoin or are concerned about security, a hardware wallet may be the best option, as it offers the highest level of security by keeping your private keys offline. If you only hold a small amount of Bitcoin and prioritize convenience over security, a software wallet may be a better choice.

Another important factor to consider is accessibility. Some wallets may not be available in certain countries or may only support certain devices or operating systems. Make sure to check the availability of the wallet before making your decision.

Fees are also an important consideration when selecting a Bitcoin wallet. Some wallets may charge transaction fees or other fees for using their services. Make sure to research the fees associated with each wallet and determine whether they fit within your budget.

Ease of use is another factor to consider. Some wallets may have a more complex user interface, which may not be suitable for those new to Bitcoin. Others may be more user-friendly and have a simpler interface. Consider your technical expertise and choose a wallet that matches your skill level.

Finally, consider the reputation and track record of the wallet provider. Look for wallets that have been in the market for a while and have a good reputation for security and reliability. It is also a good idea to check online reviews and ratings before making your decision.

In summary, when choosing the right Bitcoin wallet, it is important to consider your security needs, accessibility, fees, ease of use, and reputation of the wallet provider. By carefully considering these factors, you can choose a wallet that meets your needs and gives you peace of mind knowing that your Bitcoin is secure.

Chapter 2: Securing Your Bitcoin Wallet
Creating a strong password

Creating a strong password is essential for securing your Bitcoin wallet. A strong password is one that is difficult for others to guess or crack. It should be a combination of uppercase and lowercase letters, numbers, and special characters.

When creating a password for your Bitcoin wallet, it is important to avoid using easily guessable information such as your name, birthdate, or common words. Instead, consider using a passphrase or a combination of random words that are easy for you to remember but difficult for others to guess.

It is also recommended that you use a different password for your Bitcoin wallet than you use for any other accounts or services. This can help prevent a hacker from accessing your Bitcoin wallet if they are able to obtain your password from another source.

In addition to creating a strong password, it is important to keep your password safe and secure. Do not share your password with anyone and avoid writing it down or storing it in an easily accessible location. Consider using a password manager to securely store your passwords and generate strong, unique passwords for each of your accounts.

Lastly, it is important to regularly update your password and avoid reusing old passwords. This can help ensure that your Bitcoin wallet remains secure and protected against potential attacks. By taking the time to create a strong and unique password, you can greatly reduce the risk of your Bitcoin wallet being compromised.

Two-factor authentication

Two-factor authentication (2FA) is an additional layer of security that can be added to your Bitcoin wallet to protect it from unauthorized access. It works by requiring the user to provide two forms of identification before they can access their wallet. The first factor is usually something you know, such as a password or a PIN, while the second factor is something you have, such as a mobile phone or a hardware token.

There are several types of 2FA available for Bitcoin wallets, including SMS-based, app-based, and hardware-based authentication.

SMS-based authentication involves receiving a one-time code via text message to your mobile phone, which you then enter into the wallet software to gain access. While SMS-based 2FA is better than having no 2FA at all, it is not the most secure option, as hackers can intercept the text message and gain access to your wallet.

App-based authentication, on the other hand, involves using a dedicated app to generate a one-time code that you enter into your wallet software. The app may use a variety of methods to generate the code, such as time-based, counter-based, or even biometric authentication. This method is generally more secure than SMS-based 2FA, as the code is not transmitted over the mobile network.

Hardware-based authentication is the most secure form of 2FA, as it involves using a dedicated hardware device to generate the one-time code. The hardware device may be a USB key, a smart card, or even a biometric device such as a fingerprint scanner. This method is not only more secure than app-based or SMS-based 2FA, but it is also more convenient, as the user does not need to rely on a mobile phone or internet connection.

When setting up 2FA for your Bitcoin wallet, it is important to choose a strong and unique password for your wallet, as well as a strong and unique password for your 2FA device. It is also important to keep your 2FA device secure and to never share your password or one-time codes with anyone.

In conclusion, adding 2FA to your Bitcoin wallet is an important step in securing your holdings from unauthorized access. While SMS-based authentication is better than having no 2FA at all, app-based or hardware-based authentication is more secure and should be used whenever possible. By following best practices for password security and keeping your 2FA device secure, you can greatly reduce the risk of your Bitcoin wallet being compromised.

Multisignature wallets

Multisignature wallets, also known as multisig wallets, are a type of Bitcoin wallet that requires multiple signatures or approvals before a transaction can be completed. This adds an extra layer of security to the wallet and helps protect against theft and fraud.

In a typical Bitcoin transaction, a single signature is required to approve and send the funds. With a multisig wallet, however, multiple signatures are required, often from different parties, such as co-signers or trustees. For example, a multisig wallet may require two out of three possible signatures to approve a transaction, meaning that at least two of the three co-signers must approve the transaction before it can be completed.

The main advantage of multisig wallets is that they provide increased security and protection against theft or fraud. In a single-signature wallet, if an attacker gains access to the private key, they can easily transfer the funds to another account without any further approval needed. With a multisig wallet, however, the attacker would need to gain access to multiple private keys or convince multiple co-signers to approve the transaction, which is much more difficult.

Another advantage of multisig wallets is that they can be used for more complex financial transactions that require multiple approvals. For example, a business may use a multisig wallet to require multiple executives to approve large purchases or transfers of funds.

There are different types of multisig wallets available, each with its own requirements and features. Some wallets use a simple "M-of-N" scheme, where "M" is the number of required signatures and "N" is the total number of co-signers. Other wallets may use more complex schemes, such as hierarchical deterministic multisig, which allows for greater flexibility and control over the wallet's security.

It is important to note that while multisig wallets offer increased security, they also require more time and effort to set up and manage. Users must carefully select co-signers and ensure that all necessary signatures are obtained before completing a transaction. Additionally, multisig wallets may have higher fees due to the increased complexity of the transactions.

Overall, multisig wallets can provide an important layer of security for Bitcoin holders who want to protect their funds against theft and fraud. By requiring multiple signatures or approvals, multisig wallets help ensure that transactions are legitimate and secure, making them a valuable tool for anyone looking to secure their Bitcoin holdings.

Seed phrases and recovery phrases

Seed phrases and recovery phrases, also known as mnemonic phrases, are a crucial aspect of Bitcoin wallet security. They are essentially a set of words that are used to generate and recover the private keys associated with a particular Bitcoin wallet. Seed phrases are typically generated automatically by wallet software, and are provided to the user at the time of wallet creation.

The importance of seed phrases lies in their ability to allow users to recover their funds in the event that their wallet is lost, stolen, or damaged. With a seed phrase, a user can simply restore their wallet on a new device or software, and regain access to their funds.

Seed phrases typically consist of 12 to 24 words, and are generated using advanced cryptographic algorithms. These phrases are unique to each wallet, and are randomly generated to ensure that they cannot be easily guessed or predicted.

To ensure the security of your seed phrase, it is important to follow certain best practices. First and foremost, you should never share your seed phrase with anyone, as this could compromise the security of your wallet. You should also store your seed phrase in a safe and secure location, such as a fireproof safe or a safety deposit box.

Another best practice is to consider using a passphrase in addition to your seed phrase. A passphrase is an additional layer of security that can be added to your wallet, and is essentially a second password that is required to access your funds. By using a passphrase, you can further enhance the security of your wallet and protect against potential attacks.

Overall, seed phrases and recovery phrases are a critical aspect of Bitcoin wallet security. By following best practices and taking the necessary precautions, you can help ensure that your funds remain safe and secure.

Chapter 3: Best Practices for Bitcoin Storage
Avoiding online wallets and exchanges

When it comes to Bitcoin storage, one of the most important decisions you will make is where to store your coins. Online wallets and exchanges are popular options for many people, as they offer convenience and easy access to your funds. However, these types of services also come with inherent risks that you should be aware of. In this section, we will discuss some of the dangers associated with online wallets and exchanges and provide tips on how to avoid them.

One of the biggest risks of using an online wallet or exchange is that you do not have direct control over your private keys. Instead, you are trusting a third-party service to hold your coins and keep them secure. While many reputable services take security seriously and employ industry-standard measures to protect their users' funds, there have been numerous instances of hacks and thefts in the past that have resulted in significant losses for users.

To avoid these risks, it is generally recommended to avoid keeping large amounts of Bitcoin in online wallets or exchanges for extended periods of time. Instead, consider using these services only for short-term storage while you are actively trading or using your coins, and move your funds to a more secure storage option as soon as possible.

Another danger of using online wallets and exchanges is that they can be vulnerable to hacking and other types of attacks. Even the most secure services can be targeted by determined hackers, and if they are successful in breaching the service's security, they can potentially gain access to all of the funds held by the service's users.

To reduce your risk of being affected by a hack or security breach, it is important to carefully choose which services you use and to regularly monitor your accounts for any unusual activity. Look for services that have a proven track record of security and a strong reputation within the Bitcoin community. Additionally, be sure to enable two-factor authentication and other security features offered by the service to further protect your account.

In summary, while online wallets and exchanges can be a convenient way to store and access your Bitcoin, they come with inherent risks that should not be taken lightly. To reduce your risk of losing your coins to theft or hacking, it is important to limit the amount of Bitcoin you keep in these types of services and to use them only for short-term storage while actively trading or using your coins. Additionally, carefully choose which services you use and enable all available security features to further protect your account.

Keeping your wallet software and hardware up-to-date

One of the most important things you can do to keep your Bitcoin wallet secure is to ensure that your wallet software and hardware are up-to-date. Wallet software and hardware manufacturers regularly release updates to address security vulnerabilities and improve the overall functionality of their products. Failing to update your wallet software or hardware could leave you vulnerable to attacks that have already been patched.

Updates to wallet software typically address known security vulnerabilities or other bugs that have been discovered since the last version was released. This means that if you don't update your wallet software, you're potentially leaving yourself open to the same security issues that others have already identified and reported. Additionally, new features are often added to wallet software that improve the user experience or add new security measures, so keeping your wallet software up-to-date ensures that you're benefiting from the latest and greatest features and security enhancements.

Hardware wallets, like software wallets, also require regular updates to maintain their security. Typically, hardware wallets are updated by connecting the device to a computer and using the manufacturer's software to download the latest firmware. This process is usually straightforward, and the manufacturer will typically provide detailed instructions on how to update your device.

When it comes to updating your wallet software or hardware, there are a few best practices to keep in mind:

1. Check for updates regularly: Don't wait until you need to make a transaction to update your wallet software or hardware. Check for updates regularly and install them as soon as they become available.

2. Only download updates from official sources: Be wary of downloading wallet software or firmware updates from unofficial sources. Stick to the manufacturer's website or official app store to ensure that you're getting a legitimate update.

3. Back up your wallet before updating: Before updating your wallet software or hardware, make sure to back up your wallet. This will ensure that you have a copy of your private keys in case something goes wrong during the update process.

4. Follow the manufacturer's instructions carefully: Manufacturers will typically provide detailed instructions on how to update your wallet software or hardware. Follow

these instructions carefully to ensure a smooth update process.

By keeping your wallet software and hardware up-to-date, you're taking an important step in securing your Bitcoin holdings. Updates can be time-consuming, but they're a small price to pay for the peace of mind that comes with knowing that your wallet is as secure as possible.

Backing up your wallet

When it comes to securing your Bitcoin, backing up your wallet is one of the most important things you can do. A backup ensures that if your device or wallet becomes lost, stolen, or damaged, you can still access your funds.

There are several ways to back up your Bitcoin wallet, and each method has its own advantages and disadvantages. In this section, we'll explore the different backup methods and how to choose the right one for your needs.

1. Paper Wallet Backup A paper wallet is a printed copy of your public and private keys. This method is a popular backup option for those who want to store their Bitcoin offline. To create a paper wallet, you can use an offline generator tool that creates a new address and prints it on a paper wallet. It's important to keep the paper wallet in a safe place, such as a fireproof safe or safety deposit box.

2. USB Drive Backup Another way to backup your wallet is to use a USB drive. This method involves copying the wallet file onto a USB drive and storing it in a secure location. The advantage of this method is that it's easy to create and restore a backup using the USB drive. However, if the USB drive is lost or stolen, your Bitcoin is also at risk.

3. Cloud Backup Cloud backup is a convenient way to store your wallet files offsite, and it's easy to set up. The

advantage of this method is that you can access your backup from anywhere, but the downside is that it relies on a third-party service, which may not be secure.

4. Hardware Wallet Backup If you're using a hardware wallet, such as a Ledger or Trezor, it comes with a backup option. Hardware wallets typically include a recovery seed phrase, which is a set of 12 or 24 words that can be used to restore your wallet on a new device. It's important to store the recovery seed phrase in a secure location, such as a fireproof safe or safety deposit box.

5. Multiple Backup Locations It's always a good idea to have multiple backup locations for your wallet. This means storing copies of your wallet file or seed phrase in different locations, such as a USB drive, a paper wallet, and a hardware wallet. This way, if one backup location becomes lost or damaged, you have other backups to rely on.

When choosing a backup method, consider your own security needs and level of technical expertise. It's also important to regularly update your backups and test them to ensure they are working properly. By taking the time to backup your wallet, you can have peace of mind knowing your Bitcoin is secure and accessible in case of an emergency.

Keeping your private keys secure

Bitcoin private keys are essential for accessing and managing your funds. If someone gains access to your private keys, they can steal your bitcoins, so it is important to keep them secure. Here are some best practices for keeping your private keys safe:

1. Use a Hardware Wallet: Hardware wallets are the most secure way to store your private keys because they keep your keys offline and require physical access to sign transactions. When you use a hardware wallet, your private keys never leave the device and are never exposed to the internet.

2. Use a Strong Password: If you are using a software wallet, it is important to use a strong and unique password to protect your private keys. Do not use the same password for multiple accounts, and avoid using passwords that are easy to guess.

3. Store your Keys in a Secure Location: If you have a paper wallet or a hardware wallet, make sure to store it in a secure location, such as a safe or safety deposit box. If you have a software wallet, make sure to store your private keys on a separate device that is not connected to the internet.

4. Use Multisignature Wallets: Multisignature wallets require multiple private keys to sign transactions, which

makes them more secure than single-signature wallets. With a multisignature wallet, you can set up a wallet that requires two or more people to sign off on transactions, which adds an extra layer of security.

5. Keep Your Private Keys Offline: If you need to access your private keys, make sure to do it on a device that is not connected to the internet. This reduces the risk of your private keys being stolen by hackers or malware.

6. Avoid Public Wi-Fi: When accessing your private keys, make sure to use a secure internet connection. Public Wi-Fi networks are not secure and can be easily hacked, which can compromise your private keys.

7. Use Two-Factor Authentication: Two-factor authentication adds an extra layer of security to your wallet by requiring a second authentication method, such as a fingerprint scan or a text message code, in addition to your password.

8. Keep Your Recovery Phrases Safe: If you lose access to your wallet or your hardware wallet is stolen, you can use your recovery phrase to restore your wallet. Make sure to keep your recovery phrase in a safe location that is not accessible to others.

By following these best practices, you can keep your private keys secure and reduce the risk of losing your bitcoins. Remember, the security of your bitcoins is ultimately your responsibility, so it is important to take the necessary precautions to keep them safe.

Chapter 4: Protecting Against Common Scams and Attacks

Phishing attacks and how to avoid them

Phishing attacks are one of the most common types of scams in the cryptocurrency world. They involve tricking individuals into providing their private keys or seed phrases by posing as legitimate companies or organizations. In this section, we will discuss how to recognize phishing attacks and how to avoid falling victim to them.

What is a Phishing Attack?

A phishing attack is a type of scam in which an attacker creates a fake website or email that appears to be from a legitimate company or organization, such as a cryptocurrency exchange or wallet provider. The attacker then tricks the victim into providing sensitive information, such as their private keys or seed phrases, by convincing them that they need to do so for security reasons or to access their account.

Phishing attacks can be very convincing and sophisticated, with attackers using tactics such as social engineering and spoofed websites to make their scams appear legitimate. Once the victim provides their sensitive information, the attacker can use it to access their cryptocurrency funds and steal them.

How to Recognize a Phishing Attack

There are several signs that can indicate that an email or website is a phishing scam. These include:

1. Poor grammar and spelling: Phishing emails often contain typos, grammatical errors, and other mistakes that suggest that they were written by non-native speakers of the language.

2. Suspicious links: Phishing emails often contain links that look legitimate but actually redirect the user to a fake website designed to steal their information.

3. Urgent requests: Phishing emails often contain urgent requests for the user to take action, such as providing their private keys or seed phrases, to prevent a security breach.

4. Spoofed websites: Phishing websites often look like legitimate websites, but have slight differences in the URL or design that indicate that they are fake.

How to Avoid Phishing Scams

To avoid falling victim to phishing scams, there are several steps you can take:

1. Use two-factor authentication: Two-factor authentication adds an extra layer of security to your cryptocurrency accounts, making it more difficult for attackers to gain access to your funds.

2. Never click on suspicious links: If you receive an email or message containing a link that you are unsure about, do not click on it. Instead, go directly to the website in question and log in from there.

3. Verify the sender: If you receive an email or message that seems suspicious, verify the sender's identity before providing any sensitive information. Contact the company or organization directly to confirm that the message is legitimate.

4. Keep your software up-to-date: Keeping your wallet software and other security software up-to-date can help protect against known vulnerabilities and security threats.

5. Trust your instincts: If something seems too good to be true or seems suspicious, trust your instincts and do not provide any sensitive information.

Conclusion

Phishing attacks are a serious threat to cryptocurrency users, but by understanding how they work and taking steps to protect yourself, you can reduce your risk of falling victim to these scams. Always be vigilant and cautious when receiving messages or emails that request sensitive information, and take steps to secure your cryptocurrency accounts and wallets to prevent unauthorized access.

Malware and other types of attacks

Malware and other types of attacks are a serious threat to Bitcoin wallets, as they can compromise the security of the device and steal the user's private keys. There are several types of malware that are specifically designed to target Bitcoin wallets, including keyloggers, screen grabbers, and clipboard hijackers. In this section, we will discuss these types of attacks and how to protect against them.

Keyloggers are programs that record every keystroke made on the device, including passwords and private keys. These can be especially dangerous for Bitcoin wallets, as they can capture the user's login credentials and steal their funds. Keyloggers can be installed on a device through a variety of means, such as phishing emails, infected downloads, or malicious websites.

To protect against keyloggers, it is important to keep your device's operating system and security software up to date. This will ensure that your device has the latest security patches and can detect and remove any malware that may be present. Additionally, you can use anti-keylogger software, which is specifically designed to detect and block keylogging programs.

Screen grabbers are another type of malware that can compromise the security of Bitcoin wallets. These programs capture screenshots of the user's device, which can include sensitive information such as private keys and passwords. Screen grabbers can be installed on a device through similar means as keyloggers, such as phishing emails or malicious downloads.

To protect against screen grabbers, it is important to be cautious when downloading files or clicking on links. Only download software or files from trusted sources, and always scan them for malware before opening them. Additionally, you can use a screen capture protection tool, which will prevent any program from capturing screenshots of your device.

Clipboard hijackers are a type of malware that targets the user's clipboard, which is a temporary storage area for copied text and data. Clipboard hijackers can replace the user's Bitcoin address with a fraudulent address, which can result in funds being sent to the attacker instead of the intended recipient. These types of attacks can occur when the user copies a Bitcoin address from a website or email and then pastes it into their wallet.

To protect against clipboard hijackers, it is important to verify the Bitcoin address before sending any funds. Double-check the address to ensure that it matches the intended recipient's address, and consider using a Bitcoin wallet that supports the use of payment protocols, such as BIP70, which can verify the recipient's address before sending any funds.

In addition to these types of attacks, there are other types of malware and attacks that can compromise the security of Bitcoin wallets. These include phishing attacks, ransomware, and social engineering attacks. To protect against these types of attacks, it is important to stay vigilant and practice good security habits, such as keeping your device and software up to date, using strong passwords, and being cautious when downloading files or clicking on links. Additionally, consider using a hardware wallet, which can provide an extra layer of security for your Bitcoin funds.

Avoiding public Wi-Fi networks

With the proliferation of public Wi-Fi networks, it has become more convenient than ever to stay connected on the go. However, public Wi-Fi networks come with their own set of risks, especially when it comes to protecting your Bitcoin wallet. In this chapter, we will discuss the dangers of using public Wi-Fi networks and how to protect your wallet while using them.

Why public Wi-Fi networks are risky

Public Wi-Fi networks are generally unsecured, which means that anyone on the same network can potentially access your device and steal your information. Hackers often use public Wi-Fi networks as a hunting ground for potential victims, as these networks are easy to exploit and offer a wide range of targets.

In addition, public Wi-Fi networks are often found in busy areas such as airports, cafes, and hotels, making it easy for attackers to blend in and go unnoticed. They can use various tactics such as phishing, man-in-the-middle attacks, and malware to steal your Bitcoin wallet information and drain your funds.

How to protect your wallet while using public Wi-Fi networks

To protect your Bitcoin wallet while using public Wi-Fi networks, you need to take certain precautions. Here are some tips:

1. Avoid public Wi-Fi networks altogether

The best way to protect your wallet is to avoid using public Wi-Fi networks altogether. Instead, use your own mobile data network or a virtual private network (VPN) to access the internet. This will ensure that your data is encrypted and cannot be intercepted by hackers.

2. Use a hardware wallet

Hardware wallets such as Ledger Nano and Trezor are designed to be used offline and offer a high level of security. They can be used to sign transactions and send Bitcoin without ever exposing your private keys to the internet.

3. Enable two-factor authentication

Two-factor authentication adds an extra layer of security to your wallet by requiring a code in addition to your password to access your account. This can help protect your wallet from unauthorized access even if your password is compromised.

4. Keep your wallet software up-to-date

Make sure you always use the latest version of your wallet software and keep it up-to-date with the latest security patches. This will help protect your wallet from vulnerabilities that could be exploited by attackers.

5. Disable automatic Wi-Fi connections

Make sure to disable automatic Wi-Fi connections on your device to prevent it from connecting to public Wi-Fi networks without your permission. This will help you avoid accidentally connecting to a malicious network.

6. Use a password manager

Using a password manager can help you create strong and unique passwords for each of your online accounts, including your Bitcoin wallet. This can help protect your wallet from password-based attacks such as brute-force attacks and dictionary attacks.

Conclusion

Public Wi-Fi networks can pose a significant threat to your Bitcoin wallet security. To protect your wallet while using public Wi-Fi networks, you should take steps to avoid these networks altogether, use a hardware wallet, enable two-factor authentication, keep your wallet software up-to-date, disable automatic Wi-Fi connections, and use a password manager. By following these tips, you can help ensure that your Bitcoin wallet remains secure and protected against attacks.

Recognizing and avoiding Ponzi schemes and other scams

Ponzi schemes and other scams have been around for a long time, and the rise of cryptocurrencies has only provided new opportunities for scammers to take advantage of unsuspecting victims. In this section, we will discuss some common Ponzi schemes and scams, and provide tips on how to recognize and avoid them.

1. Ponzi schemes

Ponzi schemes are fraudulent investment schemes that promise high returns with little or no risk. They work by paying early investors with the money of new investors, rather than through actual profits. The scheme eventually collapses when new investors stop joining, and the scheme operators disappear with the remaining funds.

One classic example of a Ponzi scheme is the "Bernie Madoff" scheme, which ran for several decades before being exposed in 2008. Madoff promised investors consistently high returns, and was able to keep the scheme going by paying out early investors with funds from new investors.

To avoid Ponzi schemes, it's important to be wary of any investment opportunity that promises high returns with little risk. Always do your due diligence and research the investment thoroughly before putting any money into it.

Additionally, be cautious of investment opportunities that are being aggressively marketed, or that require you to recruit new investors in order to earn higher returns.

2. ICO scams

Initial Coin Offerings (ICOs) are a popular way for startups to raise funds through cryptocurrency. However, ICOs have also become a breeding ground for scams and fraudulent activity. Scammers may create fake ICOs or impersonate legitimate ones in order to trick investors into sending them money.

To avoid ICO scams, it's important to do your research and carefully evaluate the legitimacy of the ICO. Look for information about the team behind the project, their track record, and their overall credibility. Additionally, be wary of ICOs that promise unrealistic returns, or that use aggressive marketing tactics.

3. Phishing scams

Phishing scams are a common tactic used by scammers to steal sensitive information such as usernames, passwords, and private keys. These scams typically involve a fake website or email that appears to be from a legitimate source, such as a cryptocurrency exchange or wallet provider.

To avoid phishing scams, it's important to always double-check the URL of any website you visit, and to be wary of any unsolicited emails or messages asking for personal information. Additionally, always enable two-factor authentication (2FA) on your accounts to add an extra layer of security.

4. Fake giveaways and airdrops

Fake giveaways and airdrops are another common scam in the cryptocurrency space. These scams involve scammers impersonating well-known individuals or companies in order to offer free cryptocurrency in exchange for personal information or an initial investment.

To avoid these scams, it's important to always verify the authenticity of any giveaway or airdrop before participating. Look for information from the official source, and be wary of any requests for personal information or funds.

In conclusion, recognizing and avoiding Ponzi schemes and other scams requires a combination of common sense, due diligence, and a healthy dose of skepticism. By staying informed and taking the necessary precautions, you can help protect yourself from falling victim to these types of scams.

Chapter 5: Recovering from Wallet Theft or Loss
Steps to take if your wallet is hacked or stolen

Bitcoin is a digital currency that is not regulated by any central authority, which means that its security and protection solely depend on the user. Bitcoin wallets are prone to hacking, theft, and loss. If your Bitcoin wallet is hacked, stolen, or lost, it can be a stressful and devastating experience, but there are steps you can take to recover your lost funds. In this section, we will discuss the steps you can take if your wallet is hacked or stolen.

1. Contact Your Wallet Provider Immediately

The first step to take if your wallet is hacked or stolen is to contact your wallet provider immediately. If you have a hosted wallet, such as a web wallet or a mobile wallet, contact the wallet provider's customer support team immediately. The provider may be able to freeze your account and prevent the hacker from accessing your funds.

If you have a non-hosted wallet, such as a hardware wallet or a paper wallet, the provider may not have any control over your wallet. In this case, contact the manufacturer of your wallet to report the theft or hacking. You may also want to report the incident to the police.

2. Change All Your Passwords

If your wallet is hacked or stolen, the hacker may have access to your passwords and other sensitive information. Therefore, it is crucial to change all your passwords immediately. Change your passwords for your wallet, email, social media, and any other online accounts you have. Create strong passwords that are not easily guessed and avoid using the same password for multiple accounts.

3. Check Your Bitcoin Addresses

If your wallet is hacked or stolen, the hacker may have transferred your funds to another Bitcoin address. Therefore, it is essential to check all your Bitcoin addresses to see if there are any unauthorized transactions. You can use a block explorer to check the transactions on the blockchain. If you find any unauthorized transactions, contact your wallet provider immediately and report the incident.

4. Backup Your Recovery Phrase

If you have a non-hosted wallet, such as a hardware wallet or a paper wallet, you may have a recovery phrase that can be used to restore your wallet. If you have a recovery phrase, make sure to backup it up securely. You can store it in a safe place, such as a safe deposit box, a fireproof safe, or a secure cloud storage service.

5. Restore Your Wallet

If you have a non-hosted wallet and have backed up your recovery phrase, you can restore your wallet using the recovery phrase. The process may vary depending on the type of wallet you have, but it usually involves entering the recovery phrase into the wallet software or hardware device.

6. Keep Your Wallet Secure in the Future

After your wallet is hacked or stolen, it is essential to take measures to keep your wallet secure in the future. Make sure to keep your passwords secure, avoid using public Wi-Fi networks, and keep your wallet software and hardware up-to-date. Also, consider using a multisignature wallet or a hardware wallet, as they offer greater protection against hacking and theft.

In conclusion, if your wallet is hacked or stolen, it can be a stressful and devastating experience. However, by taking the steps outlined in this section, you can recover your lost funds and prevent future incidents from happening. Remember to contact your wallet provider immediately, change all your passwords, check your Bitcoin addresses, backup your recovery phrase, restore your wallet, and keep your wallet secure in the future.

Recovering from a lost or damaged hardware wallet

Hardware wallets are considered to be one of the most secure ways to store Bitcoins. However, even with the added security, they are not immune to loss or damage. Losing a hardware wallet can be a devastating experience, as it can mean the loss of all your Bitcoins. Fortunately, there are steps you can take to recover your Bitcoins even if you lose or damage your hardware wallet.

Step 1: Check for backups

The first step to recovering your Bitcoins is to check for backups. Most hardware wallets come with a recovery seed or phrase that you can use to recover your wallet in case of loss or damage. This seed phrase is a set of 12 or 24 words that you should have written down and stored in a safe place when you first set up your hardware wallet. If you have this seed phrase, you can easily restore your wallet on a new device.

Step 2: Buy a new hardware wallet

If you have lost your hardware wallet or it is damaged beyond repair, you will need to buy a new one. Make sure you purchase the same model or a compatible one that uses the same recovery seed or phrase as your original hardware wallet.

Step 3: Restore the wallet using the seed phrase

Once you have a new hardware wallet, you can restore your wallet using the seed phrase. This process involves entering the seed phrase into the new hardware wallet, which will then restore all the private keys associated with that wallet. The process may differ slightly depending on the model of your hardware wallet, but the general steps are as follows:

1. Connect your new hardware wallet to your computer.

2. Follow the on-screen instructions to set up the wallet.

3. Choose the option to restore the wallet from a seed phrase.

4. Enter the seed phrase, following the instructions provided by the wallet software.

5. The wallet software will generate all the private keys associated with that seed phrase and load them onto your new hardware wallet.

Step 4: Transfer your Bitcoins

Once your new hardware wallet is set up and your wallet has been restored using the seed phrase, you can transfer your Bitcoins to the new wallet. This process involves sending Bitcoins from the old wallet to the new wallet.

1. Open your old hardware wallet and connect it to your computer.

2. Follow the instructions provided by the wallet software to send Bitcoins.

3. Enter the public address of your new hardware wallet as the recipient.

4. Confirm the transaction and wait for it to be processed on the blockchain.

Step 5: Secure your new hardware wallet

Once your Bitcoins have been transferred to your new hardware wallet, it is important to take steps to secure it. This includes setting a strong password, enabling two-factor authentication, and keeping the seed phrase in a safe place. Make sure to keep your new hardware wallet updated with the latest firmware and software updates, and always keep it in a secure location.

Conclusion

Losing a hardware wallet can be a stressful experience, but with the right preparation and steps, you can recover your Bitcoins. Make sure to always keep a backup of your seed phrase in a safe place, and consider using a passphrase for added security. Additionally, keep your hardware wallet in a secure location, and always make sure to keep it updated with the latest firmware and software updates. By taking these steps, you can ensure that your Bitcoins are safe and secure, even in the event of loss or damage to your hardware wallet.

Preparing for the worst-case scenario

As a Bitcoin owner, it's important to be prepared for the worst-case scenario of losing your wallet, whether it be through theft, damage, or loss. There are steps you can take to minimize the impact of such an event and ensure that you have a chance of recovering your funds. This section will cover the steps you can take to prepare for the worst-case scenario.

1. Make backups of your private keys and recovery phrases

One of the most important steps you can take to prepare for the worst-case scenario is to make backups of your private keys and recovery phrases. These backups should be stored in multiple secure locations, such as a safety deposit box, a fireproof safe, or a trusted friend or family member's home. This will ensure that even if your wallet is lost or damaged, you still have a chance of recovering your funds.

2. Consider using a multisignature wallet

Another way to prepare for the worst-case scenario is to use a multisignature wallet. This type of wallet requires multiple private keys to access the funds, meaning that even if one of the keys is lost or stolen, the funds can still be accessed with the remaining keys. This provides an added layer of security and protection against loss or theft.

3. Keep a record of your transactions

It's also important to keep a record of your transactions, including the amounts, dates, and addresses involved. This information can be helpful in the event that you need to recover your funds, as it can be used to verify ownership and trace the movement of the funds.

4. Keep your hardware wallet up-to-date

If you're using a hardware wallet, it's important to keep it up-to-date with the latest firmware and software updates. These updates often include security improvements and bug fixes, which can help prevent against potential attacks or vulnerabilities.

5. Consider insurance options

Finally, consider looking into insurance options for your Bitcoin holdings. While insurance for Bitcoin is still a relatively new concept, there are now companies offering policies that can help protect against loss or theft. Make sure to research your options thoroughly and choose a reputable provider.

Conclusion

While it's never pleasant to think about the worst-case scenario of losing your Bitcoin wallet, it's important to be prepared in case it does happen. By making backups of your private keys and recovery phrases, using a multisignature wallet, keeping a record of your transactions, keeping your hardware wallet up-to-date, and considering insurance options, you can minimize the impact of a wallet loss or theft and increase your chances of recovering your funds.

Dealing with insurance and law enforcement

Dealing with insurance and law enforcement is an important step in the process of recovering from wallet theft or loss. In this section, we will discuss the different types of insurance available for cryptocurrency and how to file a claim if necessary. We will also discuss the role of law enforcement and the steps you can take to report a theft or scam.

Insurance for Cryptocurrency

Insurance for cryptocurrency is a relatively new concept, but it has become increasingly popular as more people invest in digital assets. There are two main types of insurance for cryptocurrency: cold storage insurance and hot wallet insurance.

Cold storage insurance covers cryptocurrency that is stored offline, such as in a hardware wallet or paper wallet. This type of insurance is generally considered to be more secure than hot wallet insurance because the private keys are stored offline and are less susceptible to hacking or theft. Cold storage insurance is typically more expensive than hot wallet insurance because it covers a smaller pool of assets.

Hot wallet insurance covers cryptocurrency that is stored online, such as in an exchange or mobile wallet. This type of insurance is less secure than cold storage insurance because the private keys are stored online and are more vulnerable to hacking or theft. Hot wallet insurance is typically less expensive than cold storage insurance because it covers a larger pool of assets.

When choosing an insurance provider, it is important to research the company's reputation, coverage limits, and exclusions. Some insurance policies may not cover losses due to theft or scams, so it is important to read the fine print before purchasing a policy.

Filing an Insurance Claim

If your cryptocurrency is stolen or lost, the first step is to file a claim with your insurance provider. The process for filing a claim will vary depending on the provider, but generally, you will need to provide documentation of the loss, such as a police report or evidence of a hack. The insurance company will then investigate the claim and determine if it is covered under the policy.

It is important to keep detailed records of your cryptocurrency holdings, including transaction history and wallet addresses. This information can help you provide proof of ownership and facilitate the claims process. It is also a good idea to keep backups of your seed phrase or recovery phrase in a safe place, as this information will be necessary to recover your lost cryptocurrency.

Dealing with Law Enforcement

If you are the victim of cryptocurrency theft or a scam, it is important to report the incident to law enforcement as soon as possible. In some cases, law enforcement may be able to recover your stolen funds or track down the perpetrators.

When reporting a theft or scam, it is important to provide as much information as possible, including the wallet address, transaction history, and any correspondence with the perpetrator. You should also provide any evidence you have, such as screenshots or emails, to help law enforcement investigate the case.

It is important to note that law enforcement agencies may not have the resources or expertise to investigate cryptocurrency-related crimes, so it is important to be patient and persistent in following up on your case. You may also want to consult with a lawyer who specializes in cryptocurrency law to help you navigate the legal process.

Conclusion

Dealing with insurance and law enforcement is an important step in the process of recovering from wallet theft or loss. It is important to research insurance providers and read the fine print before purchasing a policy. In the event of a loss, it is important to file a claim with your insurance provider and provide documentation of the loss. Reporting a theft or scam to law enforcement can help track down perpetrators and recover stolen funds, but it is important to be patient and persistent in following up on your case. By taking these steps, you can increase your chances of recovering your lost or stolen cryptocurrency.

Conclusion

Review of the book's key takeaways

As the world becomes increasingly digital, more and more people are turning to cryptocurrencies like Bitcoin as a means of storing and transferring wealth. However, with the benefits of using Bitcoin come new challenges and risks, particularly when it comes to securing your digital assets. In this book, we've covered a wide range of topics related to Bitcoin wallets and security, from the different types of wallets available to the best practices for storing your Bitcoin and protecting against common scams and attacks.

Throughout this book, we've emphasized the importance of taking a proactive approach to Bitcoin security. Rather than waiting for an attack to occur, it's essential to take steps to secure your Bitcoin before something goes wrong. With that in mind, let's review some of the key takeaways from this book and the steps you can take to protect your Bitcoin investments.

1. Choose the right wallet for your needs. There are many different types of Bitcoin wallets available, each with its own unique advantages and disadvantages. Whether you choose a software wallet, hardware wallet, or paper wallet will depend on your specific needs and preferences.

2. Use strong passwords and two-factor authentication. Passwords are one of the weakest points in any security system, so it's essential to choose a strong, unique password and use two-factor authentication whenever possible. This adds an additional layer of security to your Bitcoin wallet and makes it much more difficult for hackers to gain access.

3. Consider using multisignature wallets. Multisignature wallets are a great way to add an extra layer of security to your Bitcoin storage. By requiring multiple signatures to complete a transaction, multisignature wallets make it much more difficult for hackers to steal your Bitcoin.

4. Back up your wallet regularly. One of the most important steps you can take to protect your Bitcoin is to back up your wallet regularly. This ensures that you always have access to your Bitcoin, even if your primary wallet is lost, stolen, or damaged.

5. Keep your private keys secure. Your private keys are the most important piece of information when it comes to accessing your Bitcoin, so it's essential to keep them secure at all times. Consider storing them offline or using a hardware wallet to keep them safe.

6. Be aware of common scams and attacks. Scammers and hackers are constantly looking for new ways to steal

Bitcoin, so it's essential to be aware of the common scams and attacks that are currently being used. By staying informed and vigilant, you can reduce your risk of falling victim to these types of attacks.

7. Prepare for the worst-case scenario. While no one wants to think about losing their Bitcoin, it's important to be prepared for the worst-case scenario. Consider creating a recovery plan and keeping your Bitcoin in multiple locations to minimize your risk.

8. Consider insurance and legal options. In the event that your Bitcoin is lost or stolen, there may be insurance or legal options available to help you recover your losses. It's important to research these options ahead of time and consider whether they're right for you.

In conclusion, Bitcoin can be a valuable investment, but it's essential to take steps to protect your digital assets. By choosing the right wallet, using strong passwords and two-factor authentication, backing up your wallet regularly, and staying aware of common scams and attacks, you can minimize your risk and keep your Bitcoin secure. Remember to prepare for the worst-case scenario and consider insurance and legal options if necessary. With the right approach to Bitcoin security, you can enjoy the benefits of this innovative technology while protecting your investments for the future.

Final thoughts on Bitcoin wallet security

Bitcoin is a revolutionary technology that has the potential to change the way we think about money and financial transactions. However, with this new technology comes new challenges, especially when it comes to security. In this book, we have covered a wide range of topics related to Bitcoin wallet security, from the different types of wallets to best practices for storage, and protecting against common scams and attacks. In this final chapter, we will review some key takeaways and provide some final thoughts on Bitcoin wallet security.

Review of the Book's Key Takeaways

Throughout this book, we have discussed many important aspects of Bitcoin wallet security. Here are some key takeaways:

- Choose the right type of wallet for your needs: There are several different types of Bitcoin wallets available, and each has its pros and cons. It's essential to choose the right type of wallet for your specific needs.

- Use strong passwords and two-factor authentication: Creating a strong password is crucial for protecting your Bitcoin wallet, and two-factor authentication adds an extra layer of security.

- Consider using multisignature wallets: Multisignature wallets require multiple signatures to authorize a transaction, which makes them more secure than traditional wallets.

- Back up your wallet: Backing up your wallet is essential in case you lose your device or the wallet becomes corrupted.

- Keep your private keys secure: Your private keys are the most critical component of your Bitcoin wallet. It's essential to keep them secure and protected at all times.

- Avoid scams and phishing attacks: Scammers often try to trick Bitcoin users into giving away their private keys or other sensitive information. It's crucial to be aware of common scams and phishing attacks and take steps to avoid them.

- Be prepared for the worst-case scenario: No matter how careful you are, there is always a risk that you could lose access to your Bitcoin wallet. It's essential to be prepared for the worst-case scenario and have a plan in place for recovering your funds.

Final Thoughts on Bitcoin Wallet Security

As the use of Bitcoin continues to grow, so does the importance of Bitcoin wallet security. It's essential to be aware of the risks and take steps to protect your funds. Here are some final thoughts on Bitcoin wallet security:

- Stay informed: The world of Bitcoin and cryptocurrency is constantly evolving, and new threats and risks are emerging all the time. It's essential to stay informed and keep up-to-date with the latest developments.

- Take security seriously: Bitcoin wallet security is not something to take lightly. It's essential to take security seriously and take all necessary steps to protect your funds.

- Use common sense: When it comes to Bitcoin wallet security, sometimes the simplest solutions are the most effective. Using common sense, such as not clicking on suspicious links or downloading unknown software, can go a long way in protecting your funds.

- Don't put all your eggs in one basket: It's a good idea to spread your Bitcoin holdings across multiple wallets and exchanges to minimize the risk of loss or theft.

- Seek professional help if needed: If you are unsure about how to protect your Bitcoin wallet or recover your funds in case of loss or theft, it's always a good idea to seek professional help.

In conclusion, Bitcoin wallet security is an essential aspect of owning and using Bitcoin. By following the best practices outlined in this book and staying informed about the latest threats and risks, you can protect your funds and enjoy the benefits of this revolutionary technology.

Encouragement to take action and protect your Bitcoin holdings

As we come to the end of this book, it's important to reiterate the crucial importance of taking action to protect your Bitcoin holdings. By now, you should have a solid understanding of the potential risks and threats to your Bitcoin wallet and the measures you can take to safeguard your assets.

It's easy to become complacent and assume that your wallet is safe, especially if you've never experienced a security breach before. However, the reality is that hackers and scammers are constantly evolving their tactics to stay one step ahead. By neglecting to take the necessary precautions, you're putting yourself at risk of losing your hard-earned Bitcoin.

Therefore, it's essential to take action to secure your Bitcoin wallet today. Here are a few practical steps you can take to get started:

1. Review your current security measures: Take a critical look at your current wallet setup and assess whether you're doing everything you can to keep your Bitcoin safe. Have you enabled two-factor authentication? Are you using a hardware wallet? Do you have a strong, unique password?

Identifying any potential vulnerabilities is the first step towards strengthening your security.

2. Implement additional security measures: Once you've identified any weaknesses in your current setup, take steps to address them. This might mean enabling two-factor authentication, upgrading to a hardware wallet, or creating a stronger password. Remember, every additional layer of security you implement reduces the risk of a successful attack.

3. Keep up-to-date with the latest security best practices: As we've seen throughout this book, security threats are constantly evolving. Therefore, it's crucial to stay informed about the latest security best practices and adjust your wallet setup accordingly.

4. Be vigilant against scams and attacks: No matter how strong your security measures, there's always a risk of falling victim to a scam or attack. Therefore, it's essential to remain vigilant at all times. Be wary of unsolicited messages or emails, never click on suspicious links, and always verify the authenticity of any transaction before sending Bitcoin.

5. Don't keep all your eggs in one basket: Finally, it's important to spread your risk by diversifying your Bitcoin holdings across multiple wallets or exchanges. This means

that if one wallet is compromised, you won't lose all your Bitcoin.

In conclusion, taking action to protect your Bitcoin holdings is essential if you want to avoid becoming another victim of a security breach or scam. By implementing the measures outlined in this book and remaining vigilant at all times, you can significantly reduce the risk of losing your assets. Remember, the key to successful Bitcoin wallet security is to be proactive, stay informed, and never become complacent.

THE END

Key Terms and Definitions

To help you better understand the language and concepts related to aging and older adults, below you will find a list of key terms and their definitions.

Key terms

1. Bitcoin: a decentralized digital currency that uses cryptography for security and operates independently of a central bank.

2. Wallet: a digital storage device or program used to securely store private keys and enable transactions on a blockchain network.

3. Private key: a secret code that allows access to a user's Bitcoin funds and enables the initiation of transactions.

4. Public key: a code used to identify a user's Bitcoin address and facilitate the receipt of funds.

5. Multisignature wallet: a wallet that requires multiple signatures or approvals before a transaction can be executed, increasing security.

6. Seed phrase: a series of random words used to generate a private key, typically used to recover a lost or stolen wallet.

7. Hardware wallet: a physical device used to securely store private keys and facilitate transactions.

8. Two-factor authentication: a security measure that requires a user to provide two forms of identification before accessing an account or completing a transaction.

9. Phishing: a type of scam that involves tricking users into providing sensitive information by posing as a trustworthy entity.

10. Malware: malicious software designed to disrupt, damage, or gain unauthorized access to computer systems or networks.

Supporting Materials

Introduction:

- Andreas M. Antonopoulos (2014). "Mastering Bitcoin: Unlocking Digital Cryptocurrencies". O'Reilly Media, Inc.
- Nakamoto, S. (2008). "Bitcoin: A Peer-to-Peer Electronic Cash System."

Chapter 1: Types of Bitcoin Wallets

- BlockGeeks (2022). "What is a Bitcoin Wallet?" https://blockgeeks.com/guides/bitcoin-wallet-guide/
- Ledger (2022). "What is a Hardware Wallet?" https://www.ledger.com/academy/crypto/what-is-a-hardware-wallet

Chapter 2: Securing Your Bitcoin Wallet

- Trezor (2022). "Security Tips". https://trezor.io/security/
- Bitcoin.org (2022). "Securing Your Wallet". https://bitcoin.org/en/secure-your-wallet

Chapter 3: Best Practices for Bitcoin Storage

- Kraken (2022). "Bitcoin Security Guide". https://www.kraken.com/en-us/learn/bitcoin-security-guide
- Casa (2022). "Best Practices for Bitcoin Security". https://www.keys.casa/best-practices

Chapter 4: Protecting Against Common Scams and Attacks

- Coinbase (2022). "How to Detect and Avoid Bitcoin Scams". https://www.coinbase.com/learn/crypto-basics/how-to-detect-and-avoid-bitcoin-scams
- Binance Academy (2022). "Crypto Scams: How to Spot and Avoid Them". https://academy.binance.com/en/articles/crypto-scams-how-to-spot-and-avoid-them

Chapter 5: Recovering from Wallet Theft or Loss

- Ledger (2022). "What if I lose my Ledger device or it gets stolen?" https://support.ledger.com/hc/en-us/articles/115005161645-What-if-I-lose-my-Ledger-device-or-it-gets-stolen-
- Bitcoin.org (2022). "Recovering your wallet". https://bitcoin.org/en/you-need-to-know-recovering-your-bitcoin-wallet

Conclusion

- Cao, Q., & Zhong, R. Y. (2020). "Blockchain technology and its applications". In Handbook of Blockchain, Digital Finance, and Inclusion (pp. 1-25). Springer, Cham.
- Narayanan, A., Bonneau, J., Felten, E., Miller, A., & Goldfeder, S. (2016). "Bitcoin and Cryptocurrency Technologies: A Comprehensive Introduction". Princeton University Press.

www.ingramcontent.com/pod-product-compliance
Lightning Source LLC
Chambersburg PA
CBHW071009050326
40689CB00014B/3555